Pebble® Plus

AFRICAN ANIMALS
Cheetahs

by Deborah Nuzzolo
Consulting Editor: Gail Saunders-Smith, PhD

Consultant:
George Wittemyer, PhD
NSF International Postdoctoral Fellow
University of California at Berkeley

Capstone
press®

Mankato, Minnesota

Pebble Plus is published by Capstone Press,
151 Good Counsel Drive, P.O. Box 669, Mankato, Minnesota 56002.
www.capstonepress.com

1 2 3 4 5 6 13 12 11 10 09 08

Library of Congress Cataloging-in-Publication Data
Nuzzolo, Deborah.
    Cheetahs / by Deborah Nuzzolo.
    p. cm. — (Pebble plus. African animals)
    Includes bibliographical references and index.
    ISBN-13: 978-1-4296-1244-9 (hardcover)
    ISBN-10: 1-4296-1244-4 (hardcover)
    1. Cheetah — Africa — Juvenile literature. I. Title. II. Series.
QL737.C23N88 2008
599.75'9096 — dc22   2007028674

Summary: Discusses cheetahs, their African habitat, food, and behavior.

Editorial Credits
Erika L. Shores, editor; Renée T. Doyle, designer; Laura Manthe, photo researcher

Photo Credits
Dreamstime/Ankimo, 8–9
fotolia/Norman Reid, 18–19
Getty Images Inc./James Warwick, 14–15
iStockphoto/Adrian Colegate, cover; Eric Isselée, 22; Hansjoerg Richter, 1
McDonald Wildlife Photography/Joe McDonald, 4–5
Peter Arnold Inc./C & M Denis-Huot, 16–17
Photodisc/Siede Preis, cover, 1, 3 (fur)
Shutterstock/Gary Unwin, 10–11; Kondrachov Vladimir, 6–7; Phil Berry, 20–21
SuperStock Inc., 12–13

Note to Parents and Teachers

The African Animals set supports national science standards related to life science.
This book describes and illustrates cheetahs. The images support early readers in
understanding the text. The repetition of words and phrases helps early readers learn
new words. This book also introduces early readers to subject-specific vocabulary words,
which are defined in the Glossary section. Early readers may need assistance to read
some words and to use the Table of Contents, Glossary, Read More, Internet Sites, and
Index sections of the book.

Table of Contents

Living in Africa

Cheetahs speed across Africa's grassy savannas. Cheetahs are the fastest animals on land.

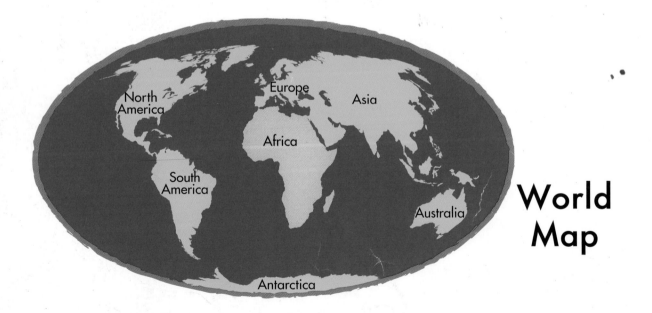

North America

Europe

Asia

Africa

South America

Australia

Antarctica

World Map

Running makes cheetahs hot.
They find a cool place
to rest on the savanna.

Africa Map

where cheetahs live

Up Close!

Can you spot the cheetah?

A cheetah's spotted coat

blends in with savanna grass.

Cheetahs look like they are
wearing sunglasses.
Black lines around
their eyes and nose
help block out sunlight.

11

Eating

Cheetahs hunt during

the day.

Their ears hear any sound.

Their eyes spy any movement.

Cheetahs chase.

Gazelles zigzag away.

Fast cheetahs hunt fast food.

Lions and hyenas sometimes
steal a cheetah's meal.
The cheetah is too tired
from hunting to protect
its food.

Staying Safe

People harm cheetahs

by taking away their land.

Many cheetahs live

in parks in Africa.

They are safe there.

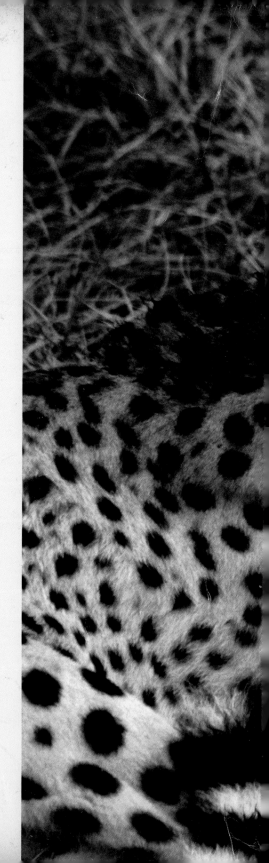

Lions and hyenas kill
cheetah cubs.
Female cheetahs hide
the cubs in dens.
Stay safe, little cheetahs!

Glossary

cub — a young cheetah

gazelle — a small antelope

hunt — to chase and kill animals for food

predator — an animal that hunts other animals for food

savanna — a flat, grassy plain with few trees

zigzag — to make sharp turns

Read More

Levine, Michelle. *Speedy Cheetahs.* Pull Ahead Books. Minneapolis: Lerner, 2007.

Murray, Julie. *Cheetahs.* Animal Kingdom. Edina, Minn.: Abdo, 2005.

Pohl, Kathleen. *Cheetahs.* Animals I See at the Zoo. Milwaukee: Gareth Stevens, 2007.

Internet Sites

FactHound offers a safe, fun way to find Internet sites related to this book. All of the sites on FactHound have been researched by our staff.

Here's how:

1. Visit *www.facthound.com*

2. Choose your grade level.

3. Type in this book ID **1429612444** for age-appropriate sites. You may also browse subjects by clicking on letters, or by clicking on pictures and words.

4. Click on the **Fetch It** button.

FactHound will fetch the best sites for you!

Index

Word Count: **139**
Grade: **1**
Early-Intervention Level: **16**